MOLOKAʻI
AN ISLAND
IN TIME

The
EARTHSONG
Collection

Molokai
An Island in Time

Photographer
Author
RICHARD A. COOKE III

Co-Author
BRONWYN A. COOKE

Editors
LIZ FOSTER
PAUL BERRY

Designer
RICKABAUGH DESIGN

The EARTHSONG Collection

Publisher
BEYOND WORDS PUBLISHING COMPANY
1221 Victoria Street
Suite 2304
Honolulu, Hawaii 96814

This book is dedicated to "Uncle Peppie" and to the people of Molokaʻi, with whom I share my love for this island.

BEYOND WORDS PUBLISHING COMPANY

Library of Congress Catalog Card Number
84 072024
ISBN: 0-681-29909-6

Printed in the United States of America
First Edition, November, 1984

I have wanted to share my vision of Moloka'i for a long time. Her elusive beauty appears in common things like the red dust of the West End, the cool winds of the highlands, the roll of the sea on sand and black rock, a greeting from a passing friend. I want these photographs to present Moloka'i as she is: unadorned, rugged and honest.

For over twenty-two years, I have taken thousands and thousands of slides of Moloka'i and her people. What I see when I look through my photographs is a series of impressions, each recording the changing face of the island and each in some way reflecting my own growth. The photographs selected for this book span the past twelve years of my life. This has been a time of learning: learning to trust, to let go of fear, to accept how things are, to give, to receive, and, above all, to share.

The Hawaiians have a saying: "When you take from the land, you must give back to the land." I hope to honor the island and her people with this book.

Following the photographs and text are a map and brief history of the island, a glossary of Hawaiian terms, and photographer's notes. The order of the chapters and pictures is chronological for the simple reason that this is the way Moloka'i happened for me and this is the way I want to share her with you.

"I had spent a good deal of time on Molokaʻi before I decided, while in architecture school, that photography was my main talent and interest. It seemed natural and logical, therefore, to spend winter break on the island, concentrating on photographing that which I had known and loved for so long. I had no plan in mind, merely accepting and recording whatever the island offered. A continuing pattern emerged right away, though I wasn't aware of it yet, and that was change: my most familiar haunts on the island's West End were caught in the drought of a very late winter, and then, while I was there, the rains came. I seem always to have loved photographing rain, and capturing the changes in the weather's mood. The search for rain often took me up into the Forest Reserve, the waterfalls and pools and lush greens of another world, less than an hour's drive from the dry West End.

"After finishing my degree in Oregon, I returned to Molokaʻi for the summer, this time with a clear goal: to photograph the deer, so plentiful, but so easily spooked that I wasn't sure it would be possible. In deer blinds I learned patience and perseverance, and I learned that I could become a trusted presence in their world; I was able to photograph the deer.

"My third visit in 1972 was at Christmas time. I was still finding subjects by instinct, and at random, committed to capturing whatever appeared to me, but now moving also toward new experiences, like the island's chicken fights."

January 1, 1972. The West End, known to the Hawaiians as the district of Kaluakoʻi since ancient times, must endure dryness most of the year. Trails made by the deer and cattle scar the land leading to the water troughs. The dry winds coat everything with blood-red dust, creating the atmosphere of African plains in a primal struggle to survive. Everything focuses on the wait for water.

January 1, 1972.

PAPOHAKU FOREST, KALUAKO'I

January 3, 1972.

January 4, 1972. High in the mountains of Central
Moloka'i is the indigenous rain forest.

January 4, 1972. At Kamoku Pool, the two-million-year-old native forest stands vulnerable to the encroachment of the hardy new forest planted by Western man.

January 5, 1972.

January 5, 1972.

January 8, 1972. The coconut grove on the lee shore of Central Molokaʻi was planted for King Kamehameha V, the last of the Kamehamehas.

July 7, 1972. Axis deer were brought from India to
Molokaʻi as a gift to King Kamehameha V in 1867.

July 11, 1972.

PAPOHAKU FOREST, KALUAKO'I

July 11, 1972.

July 24, 1972.

KEPUHI BEACH, KALUAKOʻI

July 24, 1972.

August 15, 1972. The West End, formed by the first of three volcanoes, is older than all of Moloka'i. The soil holds the secrets of centuries.

August 25, 1972.

September 18, 1972. Some places on the island feel permanent, like guardians against the wind and sea and time. This sandstone shoreline is a rugged place of jagged rocks, jagged lines. Here at the edge of the island where life looks permanent, there is constant change.

December 17, 1972. Two banyan trees frame the entry to
Puʻukolea, the old guest house of Molokai Ranch. Huge
branches, the thickness of a man's body, reach out close
to the ground, easily accessible to a child. Climbing
among the roots and branches is like playing in the arms
of a friendly old grey-skinned dragon.

December 30, 1972.

January 2, 1973.

KEPUHI BEACH, KALUAKO'I

"In 1973 I was spending nearly every waking hour thinking
of and practicing photography. I was lucky enough to begin
making a living at it and to have the opportunity to go to
India for six months. On Moloka'i, I had photographed
landscapes; but what I found in India was the people.
Although I did not yet begin to photograph people on
Moloka'i, the seed had been planted."

1974

"When I returned to Moloka'i in 1974, my sensitivity had grown and I knew that I was more attuned to atmosphere, conveying mood or feeling in my photographs, not by planning the photos, but by trusting my instinct for the moment when I saw it. I had practiced Transcendental Meditation for some time, and continued practicing while in India; I'm sure that helped me capture essences with the camera. I was noticing subtleties that I might otherwise have overlooked. I was also much more familiar with the photographic process, so I no longer had to think about it consciously."

January 5, 1974. On Moloka'i when we go to someone's house we always bring a gift, and we've never been able to leave without receiving one.

One day when we were leaving Keli'i's house, he went to his refrigerator and pulled out a hunk of freshly butchered beef. "Here," he said. I looked around for something to put it in, picturing myself driving home with this meat on my lap. He found a partly scrunched cardboard box behind his garage and shook the loose dirt out of the bottom. His face so full of love, Keli'i teaches me how to give.

January 8, 1974.

January 9, 1974.
Caught by a sudden downpour,
horses in thick winter grasses
waited behind a white curtain of rain.

January 10, 1974.
Shelter within shelter:
fog's translucent walls
in the forest's quiet rooms.

January 10, 1974.

August 20, 1974.

August 22, 1974. Barking deer; crickets buzzing in the brittle grass, and the pungent smell of lantana.

August 25, 1974.

PAPOHAKU FOREST, KALUAKOʻI

August 29,1974.

1975

"Having over the year had two gallery showings of my photographs, and having been hired by Molokai Ranch to do their annual report, I was beginning to earn my living with my camera; I bought some land in Oregon and designed my house, which I would finish building in 1976. When the annual report brought me back to Molokaʻi in February and March, I photographed mainly the West End, which was at a turning point: Kaluakoi Corporation was beginning to make changes. The bulldozers were starting to grade a road toward the West End."

February 10, 1975. Kaunakakai, the main town on Molokaʻi and home to half the island's population, is reminiscent of a sleepy town in the Old West. The storefronts have changed very little in the past fifty years, and the only indication of time passing is the newer cars. No one is in a hurry; there are no stop lights; the atmosphere is easy.

The main part of town is only three blocks long, and most of the island's business and shopping takes place here. Names on the stores like Kalama's Gas Station, Kanemitsu Bakery (famous for French bread, they also sell fish), and Pascua Store tell of the cultural cross section represented. Small, weathered homes, complete with lawns and laundry out to dry, are scattered unexpectedly behind gas stations and stores.

But the real beauty of the town is the friendliness of its people, and on Friday afternoons *pau hana* (after work), the tiny town comes alive. Everyone does weekend shopping and, through brief exchanges on the streets of Kaunakakai, the island family affirms its closeness. People wave from one car to another, "Aloha! Howz it, brah? How you stay?" They may "connect" with ten friends while looking for a parking place, five more before they get to the store. Walter stops long enough to tell me, "My arm almos' fall off! So-o-o many people to wave!"

February 20, 1975.

PAPOHAKU BEACH, KALUAKO'I

March 12, 1975. An island is a world within worlds. Its universe is the ocean.

1976

"Moloka'i, in February and March of 1976, provided material for my third gallery show, 'Amber Dialog.' A friend on Moloka'i says that the color of the West End is not amber, but burnt umber; whatever the color is called, it was a very clear influence in this year's photographs, which included some of my favorite storm weather, and my first experience photographing a fire. Although I was taking occasional slides of people, I see now that I was not yet doing the kinds of photos that would come later. The photograph of my friend Keli'i, at the end of this chapter, is more a study of light and color than a spontaneous moment."

February 5, 1976. I remember a poem* by Ross Mooney
that often comes to me when I look at certain trees:

Consider the tree,
whose fitting task it is
to inter-knit the earth and sky
in one well drawn togetherness
of soil and sun…
to make the living tree
symbol of
THE FITTING ONE
that, inter-living earth and sky,
gives birth to wholeness on the way
and gives to me
a birthplace, too,
for emerging life in me,
as I stand among the trees
and let them knit
a universe
on a Sunday afternoon.

* Excerpted from a poem by Ross Mooney.

February 16, 1976.

February 18, 1976.

February 21, 1976.

February 21, 1976. A tremendous storm cleanses the land and fills the dry stream beds, staining the beaches with the red soil of the West End, mixing the earth with the ocean.

February 22, 1976. Hiding for months, the green seems to come out in just one day after a rain, sneaking back to the surface again, life rejoicing after a long wait.

February 21, 1976.

February 26, 1976.

February 26, 1976. When an occasional fire burns out of control, it blows through the forest with incredible speed.

February 29, 1976. The fire razes undergrowth and debris, scorching the trees but traveling so fast that only thorns and limbs fall. In a few weeks the blackened trunks are covered with fresh buds; and soon afterwards, grass turns the ground green again with new life.

March 4,1976.

March 23, 1976. Keliʻi is a master fisherman, a leader and teacher of fishermen. This is his *kuleana*. This is what he knows.

1977

"1977 produced a lot of progress in my Moloka'i portfolio. Not only did I again do Molokai Ranch's annual report, I also became the Artist-in-Residence through the State Foundation on Culture and the Arts and the Department of Education, teaching all of the island's fourth graders. This very successful program helped me start to know many of the island's people through the children. And I began photographing outside of my favorite areas: I ventured into aerial shots, the North Shore, the East End, and inside Kalaupapa. Since I stayed on Moloka'i so much longer, I experienced the moods of the island, including a wonderful storm that lasted several days, which I followed from one end of the island to the other.

"The West End was changed now, but with surprisingly little change to the feeling of the land: the development sought to remain true to the flavor of the earth and the trees, the beaches and the sea. I was learning that change, as a part of life, is OK, and that beauty can survive."

January 28, 1977. Beyond Kalaupapa, the cliffs along the North Shore of Moloka'i rise almost 4,000 feet. Deep creases line the forests that tumble down the remote slopes of fern, wild guava, *'ohi'a-lehua* and *hala*. In ancient times, the valleys of Wailau, Pelekunu, and Waikolu along this coast supported large communities. The lowlands and gentler ridges were terraced to grow *kalo* (taro), the staple of the Hawaiian diet.

In the nineteenth century, these populations dwindled, then disappeared. Only in recent years have a handful of young Hawaiian families returned to live with the land and the sea in the ancient way.

January 28, 1977. Stretching twenty-five miles along the North Shore, the highest ocean cliffs in the world turn blunt faces of black and green toward steady swells rolling in from the sea.

March 10, 1977.

March 19, 1977. The arrival of the *kona* (south) wind signifies a change in weather that lasts for months, bringing the season's heavy intermittent rains.

April 5, 1977.

April 5, 1977. At first the rains are welcome to the
parched West End. But they come with such suddenness
that the land runs red with the overflow.

April 5, 1977.

April 5, 1977.

April 9, 1977.

April 11, 1977. Walking up to Moa'ula Falls at the end of Halawa Valley, you can see many of the former house sites in the now overgrown forest. Over five hundred Hawaiians once lived here, among a thousand taro patches. Today there are only a few inhabitants.

April 11, 1977.

April 20, 1977. Replacing the ancient Hawaiian grasses,
the new forest, planted within the last sixty years,
has grown up around the sacred stones in Kapale. Light
filters through branches arching high overhead,
tall trees, row after row like aisles, create the feeling of
a European cathedral. The fragrance of eucalyptus fills
the air like incense.

April 20, 1977.

April 23, 1977.

April 26, 1977.
"Fish shall come in at this pond's gate,
But no fish shall go out.
Neither shall fish go out over the wall.
This pond shall be always full of fish."

Old Hawaiian Prayer

May 18, 1977.

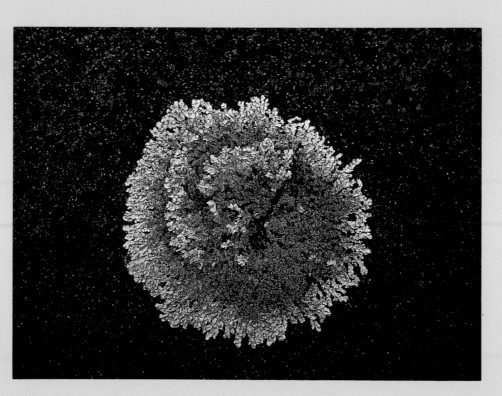

May 21, 1977. Lichen spreads like an exploding star, turning the rock on which it sits into a galaxy.

June 2, 1977. The North Shore is the most remote, inaccessible part of Moloka'i. The cliffs protect her untouched valleys, and jutting out into the sea is the isolated volcanic-rock peninsula of Kalaupapa.

June 3, 1977. Into the harsh and unfamiliar North Shore setting, Hawaiʻi's first victims of Hansen's Disease, then called leprosy, were put ashore. Having been treated like criminals and banished, they suffered most from the painful loss of their families and their homes. They arrived in an unfriendly landscape almost devoid of trees, with only a few supplies, to live out the rest of their days—five or six years at best.

Much of the history of Kalaupapa is on its gravestones.

June 3, 1977. In a sheltered nook of the isolated peninsula, residents of the Kalaupapa Settlement live their quiet lives.

June 3, 1977.

KAUHAKO CRATER, KALAUPAPA PENINSULA

June 4, 1977.

June 5, 1977.

MANILA CAMP, KAUNAKAKAI

June 6, 1977. My field trips with the fourth graders were a joy. We created great adventures together and it was on those trips that I shared my favorite places. I had never done that before.

December 23, 1977.

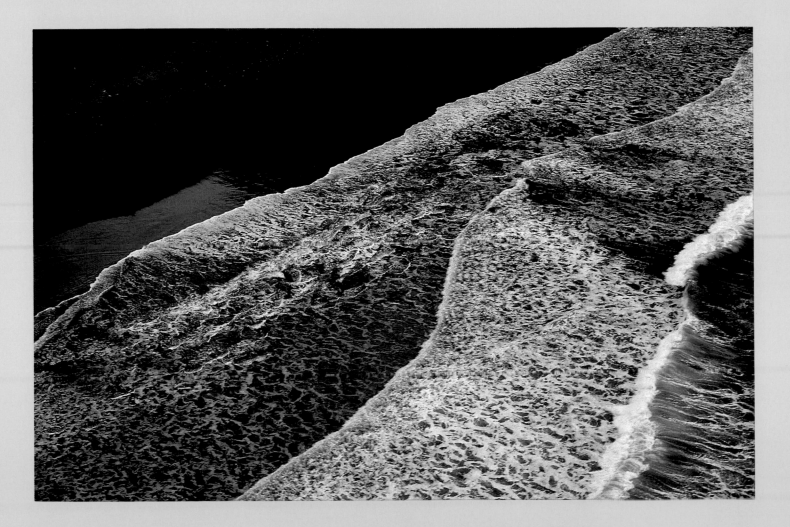

WAILAU BEACH, NORTH SHORE

December 23, 1977.

December 29, 1977.

1978

"I continued expanding what I knew about the island. For example, I met Dorothe Curtis who introduced me to archaeological sites, and to an infrequently climbed mountain called the Moʻo which became a favorite spot; I returned there again and again for spiritual renewal. I also continued taking students on field trips, which included a special trip to the sacred kukui grove in the fog. My friendship with Keliʻi grew during this time and he invited me along on some of his fishing adventures. I will never be at home in the sea, as he is, and there's little danger that I'll want to become an underwater photographer. I am content to photograph the sea's moods from the surface, and even from a distance. Nevertheless, fishing with Keliʻi and his friends has been very special."

January 25, 1978. Manaʻe ("to the east") is a direct link with the past, and for many, its preservation is a necessary part of the future. The entire East End of Molokaʻi is rich in archaeological sites. Life here is concentrated along the one road paralleling the lee shore. Driving along this road is like traveling into the island's history: here the largest and oldest concentration of Hawaiians on Molokaʻi have always lived. Signs of the past are visible in the numerous habitation sites, stone walls, and *heiau*.

Old Molokaʻi was known as the island of the *kahuna pule*. These priests of ancient times were closely attuned to the natural elements, and it is said that much of their *mana* remains embodied in the sacred places of this island. One such place is ʻIliʻiliʻopae, the largest and thought to be the oldest *heiau* on the island. It lies hidden from view in Mapulehu Valley. Older Hawaiians relate that this impressive temple was once a traditional gathering place for *kahuna* from other islands in the chain.

January 25, 1978.

April 18,1978.

May 6, 1978. From the foot of the Moʻo (Kaʻapahu) begins
a long difficult climb toward an ancient spiritual place;
a gathering spot for rainbows.

May 6, 1978.

May 7, 1978. The wind on the Moʻo rises from nowhere and everywhere, twisting, swirling off, stretching clouds into fingers, dissolving them into nothingness. Amid this antic display of power, another gust of rain blows across the Moʻo carrying a rainbow.

May 10, 1978.

May 10, 1978. The Hawaiian prophet, Lanikaula, is thought to be buried in this sacred *kukui* grove. Even in this generation many Hawaiians will not enter the grove at night, where the power of his spirit is said to remain.

May 15, 1978.

May 17, 1978.

May 23, 1978. Historically the Hawaiians used these
waters of the West End as their main fishing grounds.
Today many of the ancient roles and methods are
still honored.

May 23, 1978. This afternoon "Uncle Peppie" is the
kahu-kilo'ia, which means "the watcher, the protector":
he directs all the movements of the team in the water
from a high spot on shore, watching the large grouping of
akule and signaling the swimmers who carry the net.
A team without a good *kahu-kilo'ia* will too often blunder
into the fish, driving them out to sea.

May 23, 1978.

May 23, 1978.

KAWAKIUNUI BEACH, KALUAKO'I

"In June of 1978, a <u>National Geographic</u> staff photographer had seen my Moloka'i slides and, liking them, introduced me to the magazine. This led to some assignments for me; the first was to India for the fall and winter of 1978-1979. This time, India was an even more intense experience than it had been before, for the winter cold was bitter at 11,000 to 16,000 feet. But once again my chief studies were the people, colorful in the austere landscapes of winter. I returned to Moloka'i with new confidence, new equipment, and now with the easy habit of photographing people. During this stay on Moloka'i I revisited the Mo'o, and experienced a powerful North Shore storm of the kind that I had long wanted to photograph."

June 16, 1978. Pelekunu Valley, in the middle of the North Shore, is accessible either by boat, or by an old trail which my friend John and I decide to try. At the top, everything in the dense rain forest is wet, the ground oozey with mud. Within a half hour the trail virtually disappears; the trees and bushes scrape against our bodies and our packs. To keep our bearings we must try to keep the big valley, 4,000 feet below, on our right, but the forest often blocks our view.

After slipping and stumbling for almost ten hours, we drop down the last ridge, sliding on our backs, grabbing onto bushes where we can until we come out onto a trail just above the mossy-rock shoreline. Following the trail out to the point, we find the old geological survey cabin. In tremendous disrepair, it is at least dry, and a big window in the loft looks out onto the bay. The open ocean here is so deep that the black water moves in slow undulating rolls, the ocean so huge that I feel vulnerable on this isolated point.

We stay three days, mostly resting from the ordeal of coming in. The mountain in the evenings reaches up across the bay, silhouetted against the dark sky. The only light comes from the stars as they dance on the ocean at our feet.

April 6, 1979.

April 14, 1979.

April 14, 1979. The mountain top had once held a dense forest, but only a few trees have managed to survive. Dead *ʻohiʻa-lehua* trees stand or lie twisted everywhere, silver against the short grass, like a graveyard with its skeletons on the surface.

April 19, 1979.

April 20, 1979.

April 21, 1979. Kalaupapa is exposed to the sea and
the constant winds out of the northeast. Everything
about the setting seems exaggerated: the surf is high,
often over twenty feet in the winter, crashing against huge
formations of black lava rock that make up the shoreline
of the peninsula; the wind and rain here are stronger
than anywhere on the island; the extreme humidity
accentuates the heat; and the beauty of Kalaupapa is
magnified by its isolation and inaccessibility.

1980

"1980 was a breakthrough year for me. I started working with Bronwyn James, who would later become my wife, and also received an assignment from National Geographic to photograph Moloka'i. I wanted to capture the flavor of the island through the people; I knew I was going to have to be willing to become more visible, to be willingly involved in the people's lives. The eight months from May to December begin and end with Kalaupapa, and it is clear, even to me, that my understanding and my feeling deepened. For example, I had never photographed the patients at Kalaupapa before; the loss of that experience alone would have made a difference in my life, never mind in my journey as a photographer. The patients exemplify for me a basic truth about the generous spirit of the people of Moloka'i: when they have the most, they give the most; when they have the least, they give the best they have. In retrospect, I can see that my own philosophy was gaining new shadings as I trusted myself more, and saw the trust come back to me in the photographs. It was in this year that I realized the depth of my connection with the people of the island; I also realized that it is possible to photograph a human emotion called love."

May 10, 1980. "When we first came here, we looked at the mountains and saw a prison," Paul, a long-time resident of Kalaupapa, said. "There was no beauty for us, only survival. Over time I changed; that feeling of survival is an empty feeling. Now that we have things, I think the only way we can truly be happy is that we share with each other. By sharing, I think I have more. Any day."

"You're right," Ed, another long-time patient, said. "It's a nice feeling to give, and as long as I can, God willing, I will do it. Many people here, deep inside, are very happy," he added. "They are friendly and ready to give anything away. It's not like an institution anymore. It's like an old Hawaiian town."

May 10, 1980. The hierarchy of the Catholic Church arrives from all over Hawai'i to celebrate Damien's Day, which honors the man who chose these people and came to live out his days ministering to them. Father Damien symbolizes the spirit of selflessness and giving that is Kalaupapa.

May 16, 1980. Sister Richard Marie, "The Fishing Nun," and a nurse at Kalaupapa since 1960, says, "The people here seem to appreciate what we do for them more than anywhere else. They seem to think that we have given up everything to come. Really, I feel privileged that I've been here these years. It has been my pleasure to be here and take care of them, and to me they're just like one big family. I've gained a larger family, and I've gotten so much more. The peace of God. I don't know how to explain it but I'm not worried about outside things. I think this is a little bit of heaven."

*May 18,
1980.*

May 18, 1980. When Keli'i fishes the waters off Kalaupapa, he always drops off a couple of gunnysacks, quite often half his catch, as his way of saying, "Thank you for letting me fish in your waters." When he arrives at the wharf, people come down with pots fresh from the stove, whatever they're cooking—chicken long rice, *poi*, stewbeef—and a feast materializes, complete with beer and soda.

This is the spirit of *'ohana*: sharing what you have with others.

And this is the tradition passed on from father to son.

May 25, 1980. The softball field becomes the nucleus of
Moloka'i when teams like Kalilikane's Backhoe Service
play Dada's Body and Fender, or JoJo's Place.
Spectators park their pickups, beds facing in, lining
the edge of the field.

May 25, 1980. Men's tournaments or women's tournaments: the party is on the main street. The celebration is not of victory, but of friendship.

May 26,1980.

May 28, 1980. Seldom do you see the lee shore becalmed. Soon, a Hawaiian woman walks into the reflection of the sky, rippling the clouds with each step. It is minus low tide, a perfect time for collecting *limu.*

May 29, 1980.

May 29, 1980.

May 29, 1980.

May 31, 1980.

June 14, 1980.

KAUNAKAKAI

June 15, 1980. Cowboys and would-be cowboys look forward to the rodeo: a chance to show off skills, and an excuse to get together.

June 16, 1980.

June 20, 1980. Nelson digs the *imu* (pit); someone else builds the fire. The women make *lomi lomi* salmon while the men prepare the pigs, uncles reminding them how it's done. A *lu'au* is a time for strumming ukuleles, singing, and visiting.

June 24, 1980.

June 24, 1980. Moving the Molokai Ranch's five thousand head of Santa Gertrudis cattle each summer is a three-week task. The foreman puts out a call for all volunteer cowboys young and old, and the enlarged crew joins the adventure, driving the cattle six miles from the fields near Maunaloa to be branded, inoculated, sorted, divided into smaller herds, and sent to new pastures.

June 26, 1980. The drive is hot and dusty, and the *paniolo* (cowboys) work with more cattle than they can handle. Rounding Burrows' Gate, the cattle make a break for the open pastures; the lead cowboys must head off a stampede. As the cattle bellow, the men yell, wave their hats, and gallop through the high grasses into the herd, breaking its momentum, turning it backwards up the hill. Soon things calm down, the herd becomes more manageable, and the children take over the drive.

June 26, 1980.

June 27, 1980.

MAUNALOA, KALUAKO‘I

June 30, 1980.

July 2, 1980.

July 2, 1980.

KAʻANA PENS, KALUAKOʻI

July 2, 1980.

July 4, 1980. The *paniolo* spirit permeates the island;
you see it in the cowboy hats and in the horses staked
out along the roadsides, and you hear it in the songs of
the people.

July 16,1980.

July 22, 1980.

July 30, 1980. At home on the land and in the sea, Sammy came with his mother and five brothers and sisters in 1977 to ancestral land in Pelekunu, on the North Shore.

On a ridge above the sea, Joyce Kainoa teaches her six children to live and learn the old ways.

July 30, 1980. "The Hawaiian value says you are only there to take care of this land," Joyce says. "Hawaiians say *malama ka ʻaina*: you take care of this land because this land needs you. But do not only take, take, take; you must not destroy the soil; you must put back the seed."

"You respect the ocean because the ocean is stronger than you. First of all you have to know we have no control over nature. There is no arguing."

July 31, 1980. "The children are something like the land, to be loved and taken care of. That's why I come back here to live."

August 5, 1980. "There is always something to do, chores, hunting, fishing, tending the garden, playing. In the old Hawaiian culture the distinction between work and play was blurred."

August 5, 1980. "Nature lets you know what is going to happen: the animals, the birds, the ocean, will tell you. We rely on our instinct and our intuition."

August 13, 1980. "I just accept that the whole North Shore is part of me. I call it 'silent language.' You learn it in here," she said, as she put her hand over her heart.

August 26, 1980. A red machine the size of an automated dinosaur crawls down an endless field of grey-green blades glistening in the sun. The brightly colored hats of the crew bob up and down like multi-colored pistons of the giant machine. Everything appears to move in slow-motion. The crew dresses as if for combat: protection from the swarming bugs and sword-like leaves of the pineapple plant.

August 28,1980.

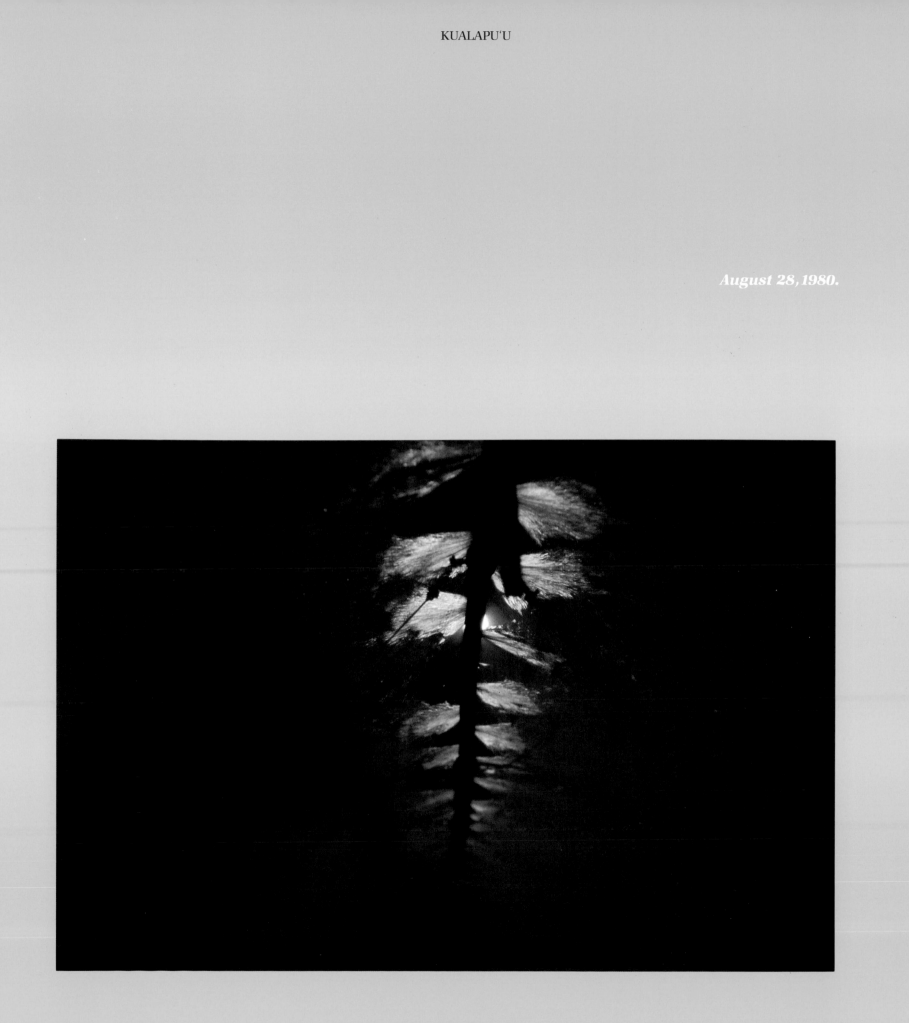

August 31, 1980.

September 7, 1980.

September 17, 1980. Moloka'i is small enough to offer the
illusion that you can see it all. The island is thirty-eight
miles long and ten miles wide.

September 17, 1980. This volcano, one of the three
that form Molokaʻi, shows the gentler erosion on the
drier leeward side. The fishponds that line the lee shore
supported the old population center of Kamalo; *ʻaina
momona*, the Hawaiians called it, meaning "fat land."

September 17, 1980. The volcanic crater's inside edges
form the sheer back walls of Pelekunu Valley, showing the
ongoing sculpting of the island.

September 28, 1980.

HALAWA VALLEY, MANA'E

September 30, 1980. There are places where the island relaxes, her edges soften, and the sand runs smoothly to the sea.

October 2, 1980.

PAPOHAKU BEACH, KALUAKO'I

October 5, 1980.

KALAUPAPA

October 6, 1980. "Aloha Week Coming!" the preview
dances announce. "Get ready for celebrate!!"

October 8, 1980. At the end of Aloha Week, the Aloha
Parade will fill this street. Everyone on the island will
participate, or gather to watch: ten floats in a good year,
fifteen in a great one; the Aloha King and Queen and
court; *pa'u* riders; a band, or maybe two. This is the
biggest, longest, most tradition-bound and tradition-
glorifying festival of the year.

October 8, 1980.

October 20, 1980. Rachel Naki grew up in the isolated valley of Wailau where her family raised taro, as did their ancestors. When her hands are in the soil, Rachel is closest to her God. As she says, "There is only God. There is nothing else."

October 21, 1980. Danny Kekahuna says he leaves his
extra sweet potatoes in the basket at the edge of his field.
His good neighbor, Moses Apo, takes from the basket and
leaves whatever he has that's extra: pumpkin, corn,
squash, watermelon. Sometimes fish. Once he even left
a jar of *limu kohu*.

October 22,1980.

October 22, 1980. The cliffs on the North Shore catch the wind, tossing clouds over these grassy highlands. As the clouds begin to creep along the ground, they hide the horizon and envelop trees and hills. Then they blow by to the south and begin to rise, returning to the sky.

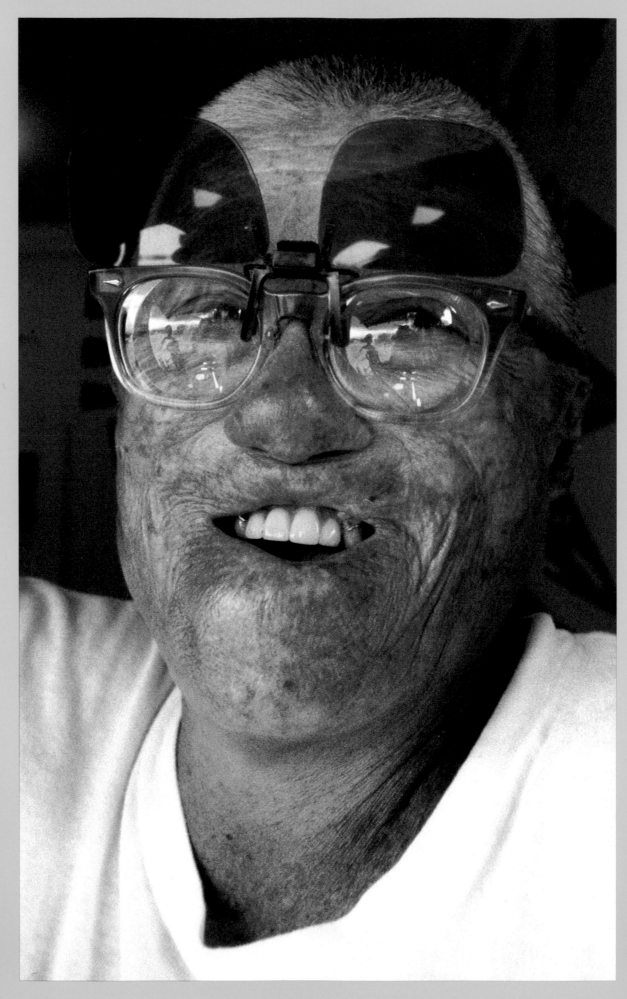

October 23, 1980. Kenso radiates an elfin cheerfulness. A world traveler, he always proclaims with pride that his home is Kalaupapa. His message is what his life exemplifies: any human being can overcome anything and be happy.

October 23, 1980. There are no children in Kalaupapa, but pets like "Tiny" and friends like Sister Richard Marie create a beautiful and necessary sense of family for Jack Sing.

November 7, 1980. She lives alone. The only links to her outside family, to all the relatives who left Moloka‘i, are these pictures.

November 19, 1980.

KAKALAHALE

December 6, 1980. The chicken fights, brought to
Moloka'i by Filipino pineapple workers, remain an
important part of the social and cultural flavor of the
island. You enter the area through weathered shelters
and coops that surround the inner courtyard. Because
the area is small, everything feels concentrated, over-
whelming your senses. Roosters tucked under their arms,
handlers move around, comparing birds. This is a time-
deepened ritual; there is a proper way to go about every
part of it.

December 6, 1980.

December 9, 1980.

December 9, 1980. If a warrior in old Hawai'i could make it to his sacred area, a *pu'uhonua*, he was granted refuge, spared. The church at Kalawao offers refuge of a different kind. The two sanctuaries, spanning time and generations, remind us that Moloka'i herself is a refuge: a sacred place where we do not seek to escape from life, but to embrace it.

December 9, 1980.

December 9, 1980.

December 17, 1980.

December 17, 1980.

KALAUPAPA

"I spent 1981 getting ready for and working on an assignment in Canada. By 1982, I was certain about my Moloka'i book, and spent much of the year working on it. My trip back to the island from February through April was planned to fill in some parts in my text. I wanted to photograph again the newly protected ancient forest of Kamakou Preserve, to return to the East End, to go back to Kalaupapa, and of course to visit the Mo'o. Most of my creative energies, though, were directed toward writing about Moloka'i, with my fiancé, Bronwyn."

February 20, 1982. Beyond the large hanging *'ama'u* ferns lies another world: a narrow, hidden valley of steep walls filled with tropical plants, trees, and ferns which seem to grow on top of each other, making it almost impossible to walk. The primary inhabitants are the reclusive birds of ancient Hawai'i.

The delicate sounds of young *apapane* filter through the stillness as the adult birds, answering the calls of their young, fly toward them in graceful arcs. In the distance you can hear the stream at the bottom of the valley. Clouds and light rain add to the illusion that you are in a time before man. This is the heart of the ancient forest, the Kamakou Preserve.

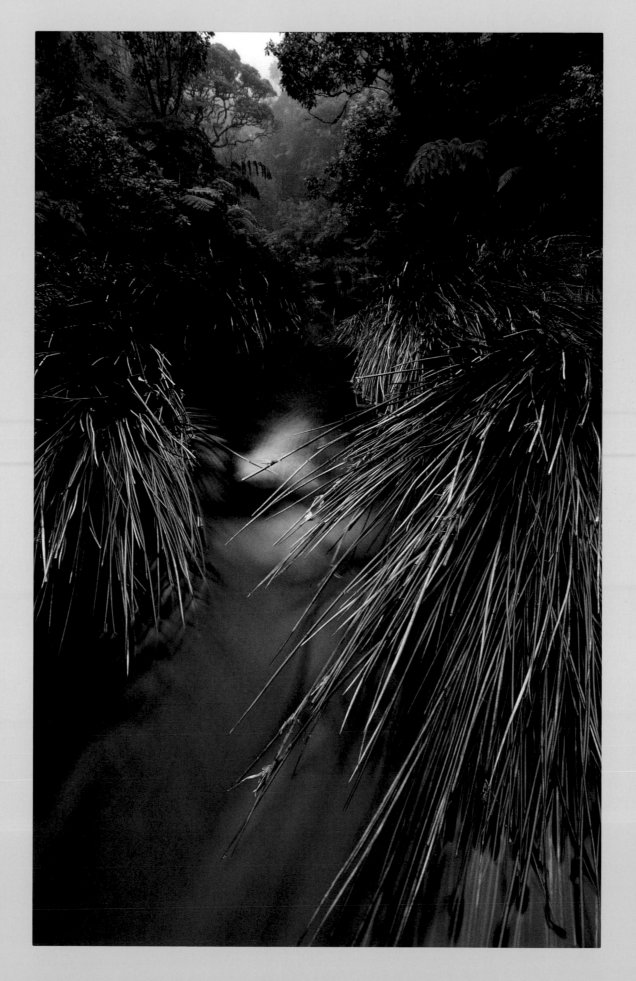

February 20, 1982.

March 25, 1982. People who live along the East End road enjoy the slow tempo and relaxed lifestyle of old Hawai'i. Folks wave from front porches, greeting passing friends; and fishermen head out along the road at ocean's edge.

April 12, 1982.

April 12, 1982.

April 19, 1982. As I stand on the rounded grassy summit of the Moʻo watching a rainbow, in the distance stands a herd of billy goats, very curious, watching me, or maybe watching rainbows.

April 19, 1982.

April 20, 1982. A white Tropic bird appears, floating from the valley on strong updrafts. Gliding gracefully with long white tail feathers drifting in the wind, it sails against the backdrop of the sea. A foreigner here, it moves closer, then slips around the ridge, and pushed by a contrary wind, floats back down to the valley.

As the distance closes between the observer and the observed, boundaries vanish. And, for a timeless moment, there is only the movement of life.

"In May of 1983, Bronwyn and I were married. When we returned to Moloka'i in 1984 it was to finish writing the book rather than to photograph. In reviewing my thousands of Moloka'i slides, and in writing about the island, I began to understand what my life and work here have taught me. The last photographs in the book represent for me the ease and joy of capturing just a few of the nice moments that come to us, routinely, as part of this place. I have learned to accept these beautiful gifts, these moments that are islands in time. It is only in the noticing of the moment, however trivial or transient, that our attention and love can realize what we see: poets put such moments into words; photographers put such moments into photographs. My experience of Moloka'i has taught me that there is always beauty, or power, or grace, or love around all of us, everywhere, all the time. It exists, whether we bother to notice it or not; but how infinitely rich and blessed our lives become when we are willing to receive and accept the gifts."

January 26, 1984.

March 15,1984.

March 15, 1984.

KAUPOA PASTURE, KALUAKO'I

"May the strength of Moloka'i be known through the pride, the joy, and the harmony of its people. May her spirit be a light, an example for all. And may this island remain protected."

Rising from the Pacific Ocean floor in Tertiary time, two small volcanic domes began to form what has become the island of Moloka'i, culminating in the most recent volcanic action which created the peninsula of Kalaupapa over a million years ago. From east to west, the island measures thirty-eight miles and has an average width of seven miles. Its 260 square miles combine ecosystems which are extremely varied—wet rain forest with an annual rainfall of 150" and dry desert land where an annual average of 1" is recorded at La'au Point. Kamakou, at 4,970 feet, peaks the major volcanic range of the eastern spine of the island; the older Maunaloa, 1,380 feet, is more gently eroded to sloping plains that form the arid western portion of the land. The dramatic, lush valleys of the less accessible northern shore and the fertile, peaceful, shallower southeastern plains create a natural shaping of the land, conducive to easy settlement.

Moloka'i nui a Hina. In Hawaiian mythology, the island's origin most often appears as the child of Hina, although its source has more than one attribution. The spirit of Hina, the wife of Wakea, legendary creator of all Hawaiian islands, is said to inhabit a shallow cave where she lived at Kalua'aha. Increasing archaeological evidence substantiates the persistent Hawaiian belief that Moloka'i holds special religious significance throughout the chain. The power and wisdom of her religious leaders were famous, and pilgrimages were common to honor their memory and to recapture a fragment of their sacred *mana*. The spirit of this strength is a prevailing influence on the island's people today.

Hawaiian tradition indicates that Moloka'i escaped the worst of the territorial battles which plagued other islands and caused more or less constant upheaval between chiefs. While the island's leadership changed hands from time to time and battles were fought along her shores, generally the island emerged as a place of refuge.

The first wave of Polynesian voyagers to have discovered Hawai'i are thought to have come from the Marquesas Islands 1,890 miles to the southeast during the second half of the 1st century A.D. Tahiti appears to have been the origin of later Polynesian journeys occurring between the 12th and 14th centuries. Along the beach at Halawa Valley is the site of the earliest settlement on Moloka'i, dating from approximately 650 A.D. Populations gradually increased and communities flourished in the deep north shore valley settings and along the protected reef-fringed shores, so similar to those that they had left behind.

Taro, or *kalo* as the Hawaiians called it, was cultivated principally in the beautifully made stone terraces, many of them remaining today, and became one of the island's first major agricultural crops. The staple sweet potato, and paper mulberry for *kapa*, were grown extensively along the *kula* slopes of the southeast end. Fish were plentiful and the shallower waters inside the reef were utilized to construct over sixty stone-enclosed fishponds of varying types, providing a reliable food source of importance to the chiefs who controlled them. In recent years these ponds have filled with silt from erosion and have been choked by mangrove, ironically introduced to control the accretion.

While the arrival in 1778 of Captain James Cook was the beginning of wrenching changes on major islands, Moloka'i, due to limited contact with other cultures, appears to have been less affected during these early years. Of greater impact was the use of Moloka'i in 1790 and again in 1795 by Kamehameha I as a staging ground for his campaigns to conquer Oahu. His troops were said to have devastated and depleted the land before moving on. The years following saw few major changes, except for a dwindling population caused by newly introduced diseases, forced gathering of sandalwood for the chiefs and some outmigration to other islands. Population during the period of first contact was estimated by Dr. Kenneth P. Emory, noted Hawaiian anthropologist, as having been 10,500. Calculations by missionary standards made in 1833 were 6,000, a figure which did not include the entire island population. This figure was dramatically reduced to 5,000 by 1839.

It was fifty years after Captain Cook's arrival in Hawai'i that we see the beginning of other significant changes. In 1832, the Reverend Harvey Rexford Hitchcock, representing the American Board of Commissioners for Foreign Missions, sailed with his wife Rebecca to Moloka'i to establish a mission station at Kalua'aha under the protection of Ho'apili-wahine (*Kaheiheimaile Kanui*), an influential Hawaiian chiefess of high rank. Soon a school and the first church were established and the congregation grew. The Reverend Hitchcock and his wife traveled by outrigger canoe to the most remote valleys to visit those souls who could not walk the distance to the church.

At the time of Hitchcock's arrival, transportation consisted of no more than canoe travel by sea, paths connecting settlements along the shore, and foot trails criss-crossing the mountain ranges between valleys on either side, scaling seemingly impossible *pali*. In 1833 Mrs. Hitchcock noted that cultural practices were strongly influenced by the past. For example, as a symbol of respect the people came before them on hands and knees, which was very disturbing to these humble and devout Christians. The old stone-rubble church built in 1844 in Kalua'aha by Hitchcock and his Hawaiian congregation is a crumbling reminder of a once-thriving community.

These first contacts with foreign culture were the beginning of an era of gradual social development and change. With the signing of the Great Mahele in 1848 and the shift in land ownership patterns, a population diversification began to take place. The year 1850 marked the arrival from Germany of a remarkable man, Rudolph Wilhelm Meyer, who until his death in 1897 was easily the most influential and prominent citizen of Moloka'i. With his Hawaiian chiefess wife, he raised eleven children to establish for his family a self-sufficient existence on the beautiful green pasturelands of Kala'e, still held by the family today. His close ties with the monarchy gained him virtually every position of authority on the island. Among his other duties, he was responsible for roads and lighthouses, schools and health, postal service, courts and taxes—often simultaneously. From the 1860s until his death, he managed the vast ranch lands of the Kamehamehas, often introducing and experimenting with new varieties of stock and grain. He also served as superintendent of the settlement at Kalaupapa for over thirty years.

The serene and beautiful Kalaupapa peninsula, which has become a refuge for so many victims of Hansen's Disease (leprosy), began with misery and suffering due to inadequacies and neglect. Assuaged by the arrival in 1873 of a vigorous and single-minded Belgian priest, Father Damien de Veuster, who devoted the rest of his life to their spiritual and physical well-being, conditions improved. Very little communication existed between other residents of Moloka'i and this isolated and restricted peninsula.

During the latter part of the 19th century, the first experimental commercial agricultural enterprises were taking place; leading the movement was again Rudolph Meyer. Until the 1870s cattle had dominated the market, being shipped live by inter-island steamers which docked at Puko'o and Kamalo'o wharves or were anchored to buoys at Pala'au and Kaunakakai. However, in recognition of the need to diversify and to encourage future economic stability, many crops were tried, among them coffee, corn, wheat, white potatoes, cotton, beans and bananas. With existing market limitations, scale was necessarily small and economic viability marginal. Present-day Moloka'i farmers experience some of the same difficulties faced by early agricultural pioneers.

With the advent of the signing of the Reciprocity Treaty in 1876, three small sugar plantations and mills had sprung up, one at Moanui, another at Kamalo'o and a third at Kala'e. Of these, the Meyer Sugar Mill was the most successful, although operated only from 1878 to 1889. Its significance to current history is the mill's survival, intact. It is presently being restored as a symbol of the island's 19th century agricultural technology and as the only sugar mill complex of its type in Hawai'i. Lack of sufficient water, in addition to sugar blight, market variabilities, and scale of operation, all contributed to the unfortunate demise of this industry on Moloka'i.

The 19th century drew to a close, and with it another era on Moloka'i. In 1898, when Hawai'i was annexed to the United States, Rudolph Meyer had died, and Charles R. Bishop, surviving husband of the last Kamehameha, had sold the lands which were to become Molokai Ranch to the American Sugar Co., Ltd. The population had dropped to an alarming 2,500, with the major distribution between Kamalo'o and Kumimi on the island's East End. The American Sugar Co. was unsuccessful in its cane sugar cultivation due to saline water in its well, and the company was purchased in 1908 by Charles M. Cooke, son of the early missionary teacher Amos Starr Cooke. He established the Molokai Ranch which, under the leadership of his son, George P. Cooke, was to become the significant vehicle for change during the next period in history. George Cooke was an uncommon man, who, with his wife Sophie, brought a willingness to fight for their principles and philosophy and a dedication to the betterment of the island and her people.

By 1920, the population of Moloka'i had reached its lowest point at 1,700. A drastic reversal was needed and it began in 1922 when Moloka'i was chosen by the Hawaiian Homes Commission as the site for its original rehabilitation project for native Hawaiians. By 1923, the Libby, McNeill and Libby Company had begun raising pineapple in the Maunaloa area on lands leased from Molokai Ranch. They continued operations until selling to the Dole Corporation in 1972. Del Monte, then known as California Packing Corporation, arrived in 1927 and made their headquarters at Kualapu'u. They soon commenced their large-scale pineapple cultivation, most of the land being leased from Molokai Ranch.

These three enterprises brought the population census figure to 5,500 by 1940. While the population was still predominately Hawaiian, many Japanese and Filipino workers had been brought in to work for the pineapple companies. The growth had shifted west, and from the 1920s on, Kaunakakai became the main population base, with central wharf facilities and electric power generation developing to accommodate the increased activity.

Molokai Ranch has continued its ongoing livestock operation while experimenting with a variety of crops. During their early years, the Hawaiian homesteaders had an active agricultural program, but the scarcity of water continued to be critical and contracting with the plantations to grow pineapple became an easier and more lucrative alternative for them. Almost all diversification ceased except on a subsistence scale.

Hawai'i's admission to statehood in 1959 as the nation's 50th state created a dimension of pride and an added degree of self-determination. The next episode of meaningful change was brought on by the final completion in 1962 of the government-financed irrigation system. With an average capacity of seven million gallons per day, much needed water is transmitted from the windward valley of Waikolu through a five-mile-long tunnel to a 100 acre butyl-lined reservoir for the development of agriculture on the central plains of Moloka'i. Once again the force of man's ingenuity has significantly shifted the ecological balance to his advantage.

Molokai Ranch runs a successful guinea grass haying operation on lands made available by the closing of the Dole pineapple plantation in 1972. Del Monte continues to produce on a reduced scale for the fresh pineapple market. As the larger agricultural businesses have left or cut back, the emphasis has again shifted to diversification, primarily seed corn, sweet potatoes, watermelons, peppers and snap beans.

Agriculture in one form or another, from *taro* culture to pineapple or ranching, has dominated almost every phase of island life. Without this base, life on Moloka'i would be a very different experience. Fishing the rich and varied ocean environments, hunting the Axis deer or wild pig, responding to personal and family relationships, gathering *maile* in the forest, contemplating alone on a remote beach or on an isolated peak—and the assurance that any or all of these are possible—make this a rather special place, and vulnerable to change.

From Kawakiu to Kanalukaha, a total of 13,000 acres of Kaluako'i land is owned by Louisiana Land & Exploration Company through its subsidiaries Kaluakoi Corporation and Molokai California. These lands were previously held by Molokai Ranch Ltd. For the first time, they have begun the orderly opening up of this area of the island to many who have never before had the opportunity to enjoy its beautiful wide-open expanses and lovely beaches. The resort facilities add dimension to the lives of many of the island's residents, but are cause for concern to those who perceive them differently.

The future's challenge is one of preservation, how to prevent the loss of traditional values and the destruction of fragile ecosystems while allowing for a freedom of choice and action by the divergent forces that make up the dynamics of today's some 6,500 residents. Whatever the emphasis, big farming or small, large developments or cottage industry, subsistence farming or some combination of the above, the setting must provide a range of individual options that do not impinge on the rights of others. It is fortunate that the strengths of the island's cultural and geographic richness combine to create an environment which encourages harmonious living between man, the land and the sea.

Dorothe Curtis

ISLAND OF MOLOKA'I

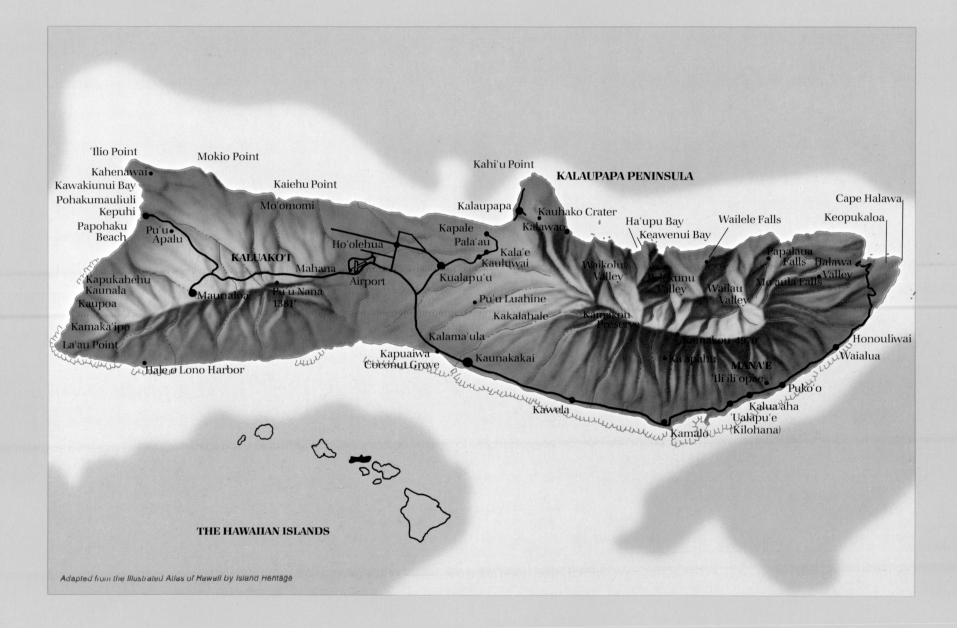

'Ilio Point

Mokio Point

Kahi'u Point

KALAUPAPA PENINSULA

Kahenawai

Kawakiunui Bay

Kaiehu Point

Cape Halawa

Pohakumauliuli

Kepuhi

Mo'omomi

Kalaupapa

Kauhako Crater

Keopukaloa

Ha'upu Bay

Wailele Falls

Papohaku
Beach

Pu'u
Apalu

Kapale

Pala'au

Kalawao

Keawenui Bay

KALUAKO'I

Ho'olehua

Kala'e

Papalaua
Falls

Halawa
Valley

Mahana

Kaluwai

Waikolu
Valley

Pelekunu
Valley

Wailau
Valley

Mo'aula Falls

Kapukahehu

Airport

Kualapu'u

Kaunala

Maunaloa

Pu'u Nana
1381'

Kaupoa

Pu'u Luahine

Kamaka'ipo

Kakalahale

Kamakou
Preserve

Honouliwai

La'au Point

Kalama'ula

Kamakou 4970'

Waialua

Hale o Lono Harbor

Kapuaiwa
Coconut Grove

Kaunakakai

Ka'apahu

MANA'E

'Ili'ili'opae

Puko'o

Kawela

Kalua'aha

'Ualapu'e

(Kilohana)

Kamalo

THE HAWAIIAN ISLANDS

All of the images in this book were taken with Canon cameras and lenses. Kodachrome film has allowed me to use a 35mm format with a wide range of lenses, and not sacrifice quality. In rain I use an 81 A warming filter, and for aerials and rainbows I use a polarizing filter.

My philosophy of photography is simple: be specific and go close. My best photographs are taken when I forget about the camera.

7 Most of the island's western lands are the cattle pastures and hayfields of Molokai Ranch Limited, the second largest ranch in Hawai'i. The Cookes have owned and managed this ranch for many years. My earliest childhood memories are of vacations I spent with my family on these lands.

This photograph shows the West End at its driest. The rains were late this year, but soon they would come, and the land would turn green again. It seems long ago now; I thought it was just a deer path. Little did I know that it was partly my own.
50mm lens

8 The West End during its dry cycle is a brutal place for living things.
20mm lens

9 I love photographing the moment of change, when sun and rain, wet and dry, combine.
50mm lens

10 *135mm lens*

11 Kamoku waterfall and pool are located deep in the Kamakou Preserve. The ginger around the pool, part of the new forest, chokes out the more delicate native plants.
50mm lens and 20mm lens

13 The 'ama'u fern, one of the many different endemic types in the preserve, sometimes reaches over six feet in height. The Nature Conservancy protects the island's oldest inhabitants, the plants and birds in the Kamakou Preserve.
50mm macro lens

14 The lehua blossom from the 'ohi'a-lehua tree: tradition says that if you pick lehua blossoms it will rain.
50mm macro lens

15 Kapuaiwa Coconut Grove.
200mm lens

16 Axis deer have been extensively hunted on the island over the years; photographing them is a challenge. Waiting in the deer blind teaches patience.
400mm lens

19 The ancient name for this beach was Kaiwiokapuhi, meaning "the bone of the eel."

The island of Oahu lies twenty-three miles away in the distance across the Kaiwi Channel.
20mm lens

21 This tree reminds me of my feelings of solitude when I am alone at night on the West End.
20mm lens, five minute exposure

22 Looking east from Kaiehu Point, in the middle of Mo'omomi Beach, the cliffs along the North Shore rise up to 4,000 feet out of deep water. It is considered one of the most rugged seacoasts in the world.
400mm lens

23 Jagged sandstone rocks protect Mo'omomi Beach from the powerful waves from the north. A huge system of sand dunes lies directly behind the beach, one of the few such ecosystems which remain in the Pacific.
200mm lens

24 Pu'ukolea was the guest house for Molokai Ranch. Hidden and protected by eucalyptus forests and pastures at its sides, the house sits below the road to Kala'e, tucked away on a knoll from which it takes its name: Pu'ukolea, "hill of the plover."

Like the banyans, the huge, one-story house, its shingled sides painted a maroon brown, spreads over the setting and looks directly at Luahine Hill and beyond to the island of Lana'i.
15mm rectilinear fisheye lens

25 Chicken fights are over very quickly, seldom lasting more than a minute. The cocks fight with a knife attached to one spur, and it is not unusual for the winner to die shortly after the loser.
135mm lens

26 These rocks are located directly in front of the Sheraton Molokai Hotel.

This picture was a tripod shot of perhaps six or seven minutes. Lengthy exposures cause some film to experience "reciprocity failure." Often a purple color will result which, in this case, adds to the mood of this late evening scene.
135mm lens

29 The Oriental tradition of leaving footwear at the door symbolizes humility and respect. It is now a part of the island way of life.
135mm lens

30 Studies show that the new forest of eucalyptus, cypress, Norfolk pine, and ironwood trees has changed the weather pattern in this area of the island.
20mm lens

31 As I approached these two white horses through the thick winter grasses, a sudden downpour with sheets of giant drops pelted the earth, soaking the horses, me, and my equipment.

My two camera bodies were ruined. The repairman asked me if I swam with my cameras.
135mm lens

32 This hunter's cabin was used many years ago when there was a problem with deer overpopulation in the Forest Reserve.
200mm lens

33 These grasses in the fog grow next to one of the reservoirs in the Forest Reserve.

Sometimes the most power, joy, or life, comes in the most subtle, quiet moments. Many times since, I have tried to recapture the delicacy of that mood.
200mm lens

34 I have done much of my deer photographing here at Kahenawai ("flowing water").

Late in the morning under an increasingly cloudy sky, as I was preparing to leave the blind, deer suddenly appeared. Simultaneously, the rains came.

Despite all the time and planning, moments like this one sometimes happen when you least expect them. Perhaps four or five times a year in brief instances like this, the observer, the camera, and the subject become one living experience.

The requirements for photographing rain are rather special: a dark background, a little sun from behind to backlight the rain, and for emphasis, a slow exposure, perhaps a thirtieth or a sixtieth of a second.
400mm lens

35 Axis deer make high-pitched sounds like a dog's bark as signals to alert the herd.

Sitting among them in my blind at Kahenawai water trough, I have learned that deer must confirm two senses before they run. These deer could hear the clicking of my camera, but they could not see or smell me, so two of the lead does barked a challenge alerting the herd.

The barking lasted for perhaps forty-five minutes, yet somehow they must have known that I meant them no harm. At times I have stood up slowly in my blind; they have looked at me and not run.
500mm lens

36 This large *kiawe* (algaroba) tree at the southern end of Papohaku Forest symbolizes for me the grandeur, the delicacy, and the majesty that I see in all *kiawe* trees.
400mm lens

37 This cabin above Kamaka'ipo Beach, one of the few buildings on the West End, was the cabin home of Kimi and Takujiro Egusa, caretakers for Molokai Ranch. After their retirement, the cabin gathered dust and finally was torn down, leaving only these pictures as a reminder.
20mm lens

39 This picture shows early morning in Kaunakakai, the island's largest town, before the parking spots fill and the people arrive for their daily shopping.
200mm lens

40 Papohaku Beach is said to be the largest white sand beach in Hawai'i.
400mm lens

41 From Pohakumauliuli Hill, this picture records the beaches prior to the changes that have since come to the West End.

Today these lands are owned by Kaluakoi Corporation, developers of the Sheraton Molokai Hotel, a golf course, and condominiums now occupying this expanse.
50mm lens

43 The sunrise highlights this *kiawe* tree in Lyman's Grove.
200mm lens

44 One of my favorite *kiawe* forests is along the road leading up to the Forest Reserve. The land responds to the winter rains, matting the ground with brilliant green weeds.
20mm lens

45 I often crouched in the limbs of this tree waiting for deer.
15mm rectilinear fisheye lens

46 *Kona* storms in winter dump huge amounts of water, flooding the dry streambeds, carrying valuable topsoil, and cutting through the beach into the bay.

On this day, although the Kaupoa road was deep in mud and water, our trusty four-wheel drive got us home.

During the rain, I used a large poncho to cover the camera mounted on a tripod.
20mm, 135mm, 20mm lenses

49 On the Forest Reserve road, the past day's rains had already helped create lacy new growth in the trees.
500mm lens

50 This was my first attempt at photographing a fire, and the intense heat forced me to use a telephoto mounted on a tripod.
135mm lens

52 The fire moved through the tops of the *kiawe* trees at forty mph, so quickly that for the most part it only burned off the outer twigs and branches.
20mm lens

53 The crotch of this old *kiawe* tree was my deer blind when I photographed at the water trough. Here, the lantana flowers were in full blossom.
20mm lens

54 The Hawaiian name for "young chief" is Keli'ipio. James Keli'ipio Mawae, known as Keli'i, is one of the last great Hawaiian fishermen on Moloka'i. Keli'i homesteads at Ho'olehua, and whenever possible he lives off the ocean and the land. This day he was "throwing net" for *moi* at 'Ilio Point. Keli'i moves with the grace of a dancer on the wet rocks.
135mm lens

56 Lilian Kamemoto and her husband, "Tree," worked at the Kalaupapa Settlement for thirty-five years.

She bought this cabin long ago for twelve dollars from a patient who later died. The people of Kalaupapa have occasionally used the place for fishing over the years. It stands alone near the point of the Kalaupapa Peninsula, where the largest waves crash during the winter.

I took this picture at sunset, when the last rays of the sun were highlighting the cabin.
200mm lens

57 Reaching out into the ocean of the North Shore, these rocky fingers of land shelter the valley of Pelekunu beyond.

All of the lands of the North Shore, including Pelekunu Valley, have been designated Conservation Lands, preserving the watershed as a future resource for the island.
50mm lens, aerial

58 The *wiliwili* is an indigenous species, and loses its leaves between July and September. Normally these trees thrive in drier lowlands, but this one stood alone in the pasture next to the sacred *kukui* grove overlooking Halawa Valley. I often return to my favorite subjects to capture their different moods and qualities. This same tree is pictured later in the fog.
200mm lens

59 The water trapped behind the beach shows the red soil after a *kona* storm.
135mm lens

60 An old *kiawe* trunk stands just above the bay during a lull in the storm.
20mm lens

61 The cowboys call this beach "*make* (dead) horse."
50mm lens

62 Later in the day at Papohaku Forest, a normally dry stream bed floods, its waters red with soil. The splashes show the size of the drops hitting the stream.
20mm lens

63 On this day, I was Keli'i Mawae's guest on a hunt through this area of Molokai Ranch.

As well as being a wonderful fisherman, Keli'i is a great hunter, one of the best shots I have ever seen.
24mm lens

64 Beside the trail to the falls are rocks of ancient walls, temples and house sites. Here the once open areas are now overgrown with trees on the east side of the valley.

Halawa Valley has the oldest known archaeological site yet to be excavated in Hawai'i.
20mm lens

65 I was unaware that Moa'ula Falls and the streams which feed it at the head of the valley were swollen with the rains of a recent storm.

Trying to get to the base of the falls, I started across what was normally a small side stream and suddenly found myself in up to my neck. Fortunately, I had my tripod extended over six feet with my camera on the end; bracing myself against the current, I saved myself from going over a fifteen foot waterfall.
200mm lens

66 The roots of the trees in this area are like gnarled hands gripping the ground. Wet and slippery, they cover most of the trail.
20mm lens

67 Some think the *wahine* stone was used as a birthing stone. This one is directly below Kauleonanahoa, the phallic rock.
15mm rectilinear fisheye lens

68 These pastures lead up to Meyer Lake, and in the background, under the fog, is the area of Kala'e. Some of the oldest pasture lands on the island, they were developed by the Meyer family, the first non-missionary westerners to settle here.
200mm lens

69 Along the lee shore, evidence of the past prosperity of Moloka'i is seen in the sixty-two contiguous fishponds, more than are found on any other Hawaiian island. Above the ponds are the remains of the terraced land where the Hawaiians grew taro (*kalo*), sweet potato ('*uala*), and mulberry (*wauke*).

This picture of Pahiomu Fishpond was taken from the head of Kamalo Gulch.
500mm lens

70 Far out on the East End road, where the number of houses starts to dwindle and the road starts to rise, the lush lands of Pu'u o Hoku Ranch begin. This beautiful pasture is situated on the plateau overlooking Halawa Valley. In the background, Moa'ula Falls and Halawa Valley are partially shrouded in the mist.
200mm lens

71 I have frequently used this picture with my Environmental Awareness Course to demonstrate the ways in which forms can interact with the creative mind. In my imagination, this lichen becomes more than just a plant on a rock.
50mm lens

72 On this evening, the light came in under the clouds that hung above the cliffs. I was able to capture the elements that unite on the North Shore during the calm of summer: grandeur and inaccessibility. The shadow in the distance hides a wall of Wailau Valley. Wailele Falls cascades toward the shoreline, and in the right foreground is part of 'Okala Island.
400mm lens from Kalaupapa Peninsula

73 At sunset, I took this picture of a Japanese gravestone in the lonely, overgrown Papaloa Cemetery just outside the Kalaupapa Settlement.
20mm lens

74 Across the street from Papaloa Cemetery is the entrance to the settlement.
200mm lens

75 This cross, at the crater in the center of the peninsula, was built by the Lion's Club in the 1950s and was used for Easter sunrise services.
20mm lens

76 I wonder what I find so attractive in abandoned cars; I guess it's that I love their faces. During 1971, I spent the entire year searching the western United States for dead cars left in the environment.
20mm lens

77 This little girl lived in one of the houses in Manila Camp next to where chicken fights were once held.
135mm lens

78 These children were part of my environmental awareness program, "Seeing Moloka'i," which I taught for three years at all the schools on the island.

The background of the picture shows the far side of Halawa Valley.
200mm lens

79 Shore break on the black sand beach at Wailau.
50mm lens, helicopter

80 The black indentations at the edges of the sections are piles of pineapple shoots which the crew leaves there for the day's planting. They place the shoots right through the plastic into the earth. With its drip irrigation, hybrid development, and advanced cultivation techniques, this Del Monte plantation is a model for the industry.
50mm lens, helicopter

81 The *kiawe* tree is known in the southwestern United States as mesquite. At sunset, shadows hide the lush Kaluakoi Golf Course in the foreground.
400mm lens

83 This *heiau* is made up of four terraces, the largest about the size of a football field. Because it is on private land, it is seldom visited and therefore is preserved. It is said that the pit in the foreground (one of several) was used to hold the bones from sacrifices, some of them human. Its purpose was to retain the *mana* (spirit) in this sacred place.
20mm lens

84 A pineapple-watering machine crawls like a snail through the fields, highlighted by the late afternoon sun. For the most part, drip irrigation has replaced these machines.
400mm lens

85 The mountain of Ka'apahu, familiarly known as the Mo'o, is located near the center of the island, adjacent to Kamalo Gulch. Directly behind the Mo'o, the impenetrable forests culminate at Kamakou, the highest point on Moloka'i.

The legend of the Mo'o tells of the territorial battle between the *mano* (shark) and the *mo'o* (lizard). Both were *'aumakua* (family or personal gods), which protected adjoining areas on the East End.

One day, the shark challenged the lizard to a battle for the domination of these lands. In the nearby shallows of the sea, they fought a day-long battle, and toward evening the lizard lay unconscious and bleeding. Believing himself to be the victor, the *mano* swam away, returning to his home in the sea at Kainalu.

The *mo'o* revived, crawled to the mountain slopes overlooking her lands and died. She became the mountain, and it is said that the western slopes are strewn with the reddish dust of her dried blood. Her spirit has lingered to protect her domain.

This was my first trip up the Mo'o, and as far as I knew, nobody had been up there in years. There was no trail so I just followed the ridge, not even certain that I could ascend the last part. From below I could not see passage to the top. When you start at sea level, walking up almost 4,000 feet feels like a long, hard hike. All the while, on what appeared to be the crest of the mountain, I could see rocks that looked like three people sitting there watching my progress as I climbed. In a way, it helped me feel less alone. I nicknamed them See No Evil, Hear No Evil, and Speak No Evil; three "monkeys" sitting on a ledge.

The top of the Mo'o is a demanding place where the different winds meet. It always seems to be raining here, and at times the wind is hard enough to blow me over. It is here that I discovered that when I let go of my fear, when I accept what is, then I can most fully give myself to the moment.
17mm lens

86 The exposed rocks show the erosion caused by the winds and the rains on top of the Mo'o. There always seems to be a rainbow floating somewhere near here. To emphasize the colors, I use a polarizing filter when photographing rainbows.
24mm lens

87 These *'ohi'a-lehua* trees, once part of a larger forest, are silhouetted against the rolling hills below. Feral goats, introduced by man, have caused tremendous change here. They eat the bark off the trees, leaving them to die, and strip any remaining ground cover that has protected this place from erosion.
200mm lens

88 My old friend the *wiliwili* tree shows me another of its many moods.
200mm lens

89 *Ulu Kukui O Lanikaula* means "the *kukui* grove of Lanikaula." This sacred stand of trees honors the prophet Lanikaula.
20mm lens

90 One of my students runs back to the bus at the end of a field trip.
200mm lens

91 Randy Manaba, one of my students from Kaunakakai School, looks under the waterfall at Kawela Intake.
24mm lens

92 For any fisherman, catching *akule* is a big score. On top of the ocean, a faint purple spot discloses their location. Actually, the fish group together to form a "pile," which is a solid column of fish from the top of the ocean all the way to its floor. On this day, we surrounded them in what might be called the "old-fashioned" way: we swam out with the nets on two inner tubes and encircled the fish completely. We ended up with around a thousand pounds of fish.
20mm lens

93 Uncle Peppie Cooke: whenever I needed help or advice, Uncle Peppie always had the answer. In many ways Peppie and his wife Pat have been my Moloka'i parents. They have overseen the creation and birth of this book.
85mm lens

94 The real work begins when the fish are caught. It takes hours to clean the nets. Here a young boy performs the work with chopsticks, untangling the fish that have been caught in the net.
85mm lens

95 Fishing is an essential part of the Hawaiian culture.
24mm lens

96 These green, mossy rocks mark the entrance of Pelekunu Stream into Pelekunu Bay. The rough waters here make it impossible for the shoreline to hold sand.
17mm lens

98 At a party celebrating her retirement as manager of Bank of Hawaii on Moloka'i, Pearl Petro, a descendant of settlers from the 19th century, greets the guests.

She wears thousands of orange 'ilima petals strung into *leis*, representing countless hours of work by her friends. The 'ilima lei symbolized royalty in old Hawai'i. The strands of fragrant green leaves beneath are *maile lauli'ili'i*, a *lei* of Moloka'i. *Maile* vines grow only on bushes and trees high in the remote native forest.
85mm lens

99 At sunset, looking through the rain, these old 'ohi'a-lehua trees are silhouetted against the lee shore of the island. In the distance is La'au Point.
200mm lens

100 Atop the Mo'o, this old 'ohi'a-lehua marks the place where a forest once stood. In the distance is the island of Lana'i.
17mm lens

101 Remnants of the old Kalawao Settlement, ironwood, *kiawe* and palm trees struggle for survival amid the ground cover that has taken over the pastures.
85mm lens

102 Technically the most unusual in the book, this photograph was taken with an anamorphic lens. Used on the front of the 85mm lens, the anamorphic attachment compresses the image and makes everything appear more vertical.
85mm lens with an anamorphic attachment

103 This is an early morning storm from Kalawao.
200mm lens with an anamorphic attachment

105 On this point stands one of the few remaining old-fashioned lighthouses in Hawai'i, now automated, and still in operation.
50mm lens

106 In Saint Philomena Church, Bishop Ferrari conducts mass for Damien's Day.
85mm lens and high-speed Ektachrome film

107 Sister Richard Marie enjoys her favorite pastime. Inspired by the dedication of Sister Marianne, who spent her life at Kalaupapa, Sister Richard Marie joined the Franciscan Order and asked to be transferred to the Settlement. After twenty years of waiting, she received the assignment here, achieving her dream.
17mm lens, copyright National Geographic Society

108 Keli'i, carrying his *akule* nets in from what is commonly known as Dixie Maru Beach. This photograph was taken by my ten-year-old son Blake, who outshot me on this day.
50mm lens

109 Junior Mawae, Keli'i's oldest son, braves a huge wave as he attempts to collect *opihi*, tiny shelled creatures that live on the rocks in a dangerous area right along the surf line. *Opihi*, considered a delicacy by the local people, are eaten raw. This photograph was taken by my wife, Bronwyn.
135mm lens

110 "Dada's Body and Fender" and the "Nawahine Wildcats" party after the Paleka Softball Tournament. Bill Kaaihue performs on the ukulele.
24mm lens

111 Annette Dela Cruz Pauole performs a spontaneous *hula* after her team, the "Wildcats," took second place in this inter-island softball tournament in Kaunakakai.
85mm lens, copyright National Geographic Society

112 A window in McVeigh Hall, an unused building, looks out over the settlement.
17mm lens

113 The wharf where I stood for this shot is one of the island's connections to the outside world. On a typical day, pineapple trucks arrive, drop their crates of fruit, and return to the fields for more. Fishermen leave the marina in search of a day's catch. Twice a week barges from Honolulu arrive with food and supplies for the island.
85mm lens

114 Students from Kilohana School sit patiently in their *holoku*, a formal version of the *mu'umu'u*. For the May Day Pageant, each girl was dressed as a different Hawaiian queen.
85mm lens

115 Stephanie Pezel is dressed as Princess Ka'ahumanu.
300mm lens

116 Lorna Bongalon Ashlock was part of a group of high school students who were working in a taro patch alongside the East End road. Their mud fight was just too much to pass up. For me, photographing it was more fun than being in the mud fight itself.
85mm lens

117 Many years ago, a fishing boat named The Dixie Maru went down in the bay adjoining Kapukahehu. When remnants were washed ashore, what had been called Kapukahehu for centuries was nicknamed Dixie Maru Bay. The mud shows the incredible color of the soil of the West End.
17mm lens

118 At the Kamehameha Day Rodeo, sponsored by the Molokai Roping Club, Earl Pawn straddles a palomino. He is introduced at the rodeos as the "Charles Bronson" of Moloka'i, and is considered one of the great hunters on the island.
135mm lens

119 The blurred image shows the team of Rena Dudoit and Guy Naehu in the calf-roping competition. The participants far outnumber the spectators. There is no admission and no grandstand; to watch you can lean against the fence or sit in your pickup.
85mm lens

120 Born in 1902, Ropo Tanaid came from the Philippines in 1923, and worked thirty-six years for Molokai Ranch. Ropo was blessed with incredible strength and was famous for his tree-climbing ability. He retired from the ranch in 1967 and now makes throw nets.
85mm lens

121 "Kalua pig" is the supreme delicacy at a traditional *lu'au*. The Ainoa family was preparing these pigs for a wedding *lu'au*, which would be held the next day. It takes a tremendous group effort and many hours to complete the preparations.
50mm lens

122 Charlie "Spooks" Wahenui typifies the happy-go-lucky nature of the hard-working cowboys of Molokai Ranch.
85mm lens

123 Having already traveled quite a distance, the cattle here move slowly on a hot afternoon. The telephoto lens used for this picture makes the background appear closer.
300mm lens

124 *17mm lens*

125 The blue in the background of this picture is the ocean.
400mm lens

126 Father and son.
200mm lens

127 Brookie Pua'a is one of the children working with the cowboys during the summer.
135mm lens

128 James Duvauchelle is the foreman for Molokai Ranch.
135mm lens

129 "Goat" Dudoit rides a heifer down the cattle chute at Ka'ana pens.
24mm lens

130 Tired and covered with dirt, "Goat" and "Spooks" embody cowboy life on Moloka'i.
24mm lens

131 For me, this is the spirit of Moloka'i, as Earl Paleka jams with workers who were preparing a *lu'au* for the Duvauchelle family reunion.
85mm lens

132 Phillip Kalipi was in charge of a project to teach students the ancient way of raising taro. Although I caught him in a pensive moment, he generally has a huge smile on his face.
135mm lens

133 Dukie Kalipi, whose father Phillip is pictured on the opposite page, takes a break during the day's work in clearing a new taro patch.
85mm lens

134 To visit Joyce Kainoa's home on the North Shore, we arrive by boat. The shoreline is too rough for a dock, so Sammy swims out to greet us with a tub to carry our baggage, leaving us free to swim ashore.

Joyce Kainoa loves to have visitors share their knowledge with her family. When you are a guest in their house, you sleep on the same floor as everybody else; they just pull out a few more foam pads.
135mm lens

135 *85mm lens*

136 The children play at Waiohoʻokalo Stream waterfall in the valley adjacent to their home.
24mm lens

137 Joyce and daughter Alice prepared dinner in the cooking extension of the house.
24mm lens

138 Sammy looks out at the twilight. We had just been fishing and had caught lobster and squid for dinner.
139mm lens, copyright National Geographic Society

139 This picture looks toward Waikolu Valley, adjacent to the Kalaupapa Peninsula.
85mm lens

140 *500mm lens*

141 Under the boom of a pineapple-watering machine, the night lights dramatize the spray.
85mm lens

142 Wearing a hat made by his wife, Danny Kekahuna kicks back at the end of the day. He is one of the few people who still speak fluent Hawaiian.
85mm lens

143 Built by George Cooke, the last of the old houses on the ranch land of the West End has been turned over to Molokai Ranch and is used as a guest house for stockholders.
50mm lens, aerial

144 This picture was taken just after sunrise, looking across Molokaʻi at Maui in the distance. Haleakala Crater looms at the back of the picture.
50mm lens, aerial at 11,500 feet

145 The top of this photograph shows the collapsed dome of the East Molokaʻi Volcano. Livestock and feral goats that graze along the heights have caused severe erosion which has filled the fishponds below. Mangrove trees, recent arrivals here, have spread through the ponds, making almost all of them useless.
24mm lens with polarizing filter, aerial

146 Stretching along the East End, the "spine" of Molokaʻi includes the highest point of Kamakou, 4,970 feet. The light-green areas at the bottom of the valley show large *kukui* trees in Pelekunu Valley.
24mm lens with polarizing filter, aerial

147 Alice Namakaeha eats a guava in Halawa Stream. She was living with her grandfather; this pool was in their backyard.

When the ancient Hawaiians lived in Halawa, there were no trees on this valley floor.
24mm lens

148 The winter surf at Papohaku Beach is often treacherous.
400mm lens, copyright National Geographic Society

149 From the south end of the beach at twilight, this picture was taken with just over a five minute exposure, blurring the waves.
400mm lens

150 Lenora Dudoit, one of the lead dancers of Moana's Dance Troupe of Molokaʻi, was waiting for the plane at Kalaupapa where she had been sharing Aloha Week festivities with the patients.
85mm lens

151 Moana's Dance Troupe performs in the heart of downtown Kaunakakai. Emcee "Butchie" Dudoit, at right, is one of the guiding forces behind the troupe.
300mm lens, copyright National Geographic Society

152 During Aloha Week, the dancers performed each day for half an hour. The relaxed manner in which they presented the program typifies the way things are often done on Molokaʻi.
24mm lens

153 Lenora Dudoit.
300mm lens

154 At the time this picture was taken, Rachel was seventy-seven. Although her pace has slowed a bit, she still works most of every day. In recent years, she and her husband, Imu, had restored the lush taro patch seen in the background. Imu has since passed away, but Rachel continues to teach the traditions of growing taro to her grandchildren.
24mm lens

155 Danny and Louise Kekahuna stand in the fertile red fields where they grow sweet potatoes to be sold to markets in Honolulu. Louise makes the island's best *lauhala* hats, and Danny makes the most soulful Hawaiian music you will hear anywhere.
24mm lens

156 These pastures above Meyer Lake look back over the west of the island. You can see Kaluakoʻi Hill silhouetted in the distance.
50mm lens

157 ʻIlio Point is visible off in the distance.
50mm lens

158 Kenso's life is quiet. Every morning he and one of his buddies watch the plane arrive. He is the altar boy at the Catholic church and often cooks meals for other bachelors who come to his house. He also handles many orders for the coconut lamps that he hand-carves and etches in his workshop. Kenso was the first patient who allowed me to photograph him. His life is such an example for me, it would be my loss not to know this man.
24mm lens

159 Since this picture was taken, both Jack Sing and his wife have died. Smiling in the background is Sister Richard Marie, a friend to all.
24mm lens

160 When this photo was taken, Jenny Kamakahi was in her eighties, living alone with just her cats and these pictures. Since then she has moved to Honolulu, following the path of younger people who have left the island of their birth.
50mm lens

161 Trying to photograph near a swarm of bees tests your courage.

For a brief time in the 1920s, Molokaʻi was the honey capital of America, shipping up to three hundred tons a year until an epidemic destroyed the bees. Today, the Italian bees of Molokai Ranch alone produce fifty tons of *kiawe* honey a year.
24mm lens

162 Ben, a retired carpenter, and two spectators enjoy the chicken fights.
85mm lens

163 With permission, I took this picture from the roof overlooking the fights.
24mm lens

164 This *puʻuhonua* (sanctuary) is located not far from the lowlands where some of the major battles of Molokaʻi were fought.
24mm lens, helicopter

165 Siloama Church was part of the original settlement at Kalawao. The weather here was too harsh, and early in this century the residents moved to the present settlement at Kalaupapa on the lee shore of the peninsula.
24mm lens, helicopter

166 At the head of Papalaua Valley, close to the east end of the North Shore, the falls drop 1,200 feet to the ocean below.
17mm lens, helicopter

167 Looking at the rough seas of winter, you can see why the barge comes in with supplies only twice a year.
24mm lens, helicopter

168 Rev. Elmer Wilson, a past administrator of the Kalaupapa Settlement and the minister in Halawa Valley, entertains at the annual Lion's Club Christmas party.
24mm lens, flash

169 Benediction.
85mm lens and high-speed Ektachrome film

171 The waters at Kawela Intake supply water to Molokai Ranch.
17mm lens

172 *'Ohi'a-lehua* trees line the trail to Kawela Intake in the heart of the Kamakou Preserve. In 1982 the State of Hawai'i, Molokai Ranch, and the Nature Conservancy acted to dedicate a 2,774-acre area of mountainous native forest, preserving an ecosystem dating back millions of years.

The forest contains 250 kinds of Hawaiian plants, 219 of them endemic to Hawai'i, and five endangered species of native birds, two of which are found only on Moloka'i. The Nature Conservancy now oversees this part of the natural heritage of Hawai'i.
24mm lens

173 Behind this shack at Kamalo Ranch on the East End, ridges rise to form the backbone of Moloka'i. At the upper left is Ka'apahu, also known as the Mo'o.
85mm lens

174 In front of the Kalaupapa store, Kenso sits in this Model-A he built out of two cars.
17mm lens

175 Postman and friends.
135mm lens

176 On yet another pilgrimage to the top of the Mo'o, I was greeted by a herd of billy goats. They did not know quite what to make of me. Behind them one can see the lines of trails on the cliff in Kamalo Gulch, and some of the erosion they have caused.
200mm lens

177 It is not often that there is a calm and clear night on top of the Mo'o. Looking back along the lee shore, one sees the lights of Kaunakakai and the wharf.
200mm lens

178 I have always camped just below this beautiful *'ohi'a-lehua* tree, one of the last living trees atop the Mo'o. On my last trip I discovered that the tree had been chopped down.
200mm lens

180 *14mm lens*

181 In the late afternoon light we could see the storm coming our way from the east carrying this rainbow to Egusa Gate. When you walk with a rainbow, the rainbow moves with you.
85mm lens

182 The storm reaches my favorite tree in the Kaupoa Pasture; the openness here reminds me that the West End is a place where my spirit always feels free.

183 Ke ana o Hina (the cave of Hina) is one of the most sacred ancient spots on Moloka'i. Small, hidden, and nondescript, the cave is said to have been the home of Hina, Mother of Moloka'i (Moloka'i nui a Hina).

It is still believed that when you visit this cave, all that is truly Moloka'i is revealed to you.

This was part of a prayer to Mother Hina on my last visit to the cave.

Abbott, Isabella Aiona and Eleanor Horswill Williamson.
Limu, An Ethnobotanical Study of Some Edible Hawaiian Seaweeds.
Kauai, Hawai'i, Pacific Tropical Botanical Gardens, 1974.

Beckwith, Martha Warren.
Hawaiian Mythology.
New Haven, Connecticut, Yale University Press, 1940.

Berger, Andrew J.
Hawaiian Birdlife.
Honolulu, University Press of Hawai'i, 1972.

Bushnell, O.A. and others.
The Illustrated Atlas of Hawai'i.
Norfolk Island, Australia, Island Heritage Limited, 1970, p. 42.

Cooke, George Paul.
Mo'olelo O Moloka'i: A Ranch Story of Moloka'i
Hawai'i, Honolulu Star-Bulletin, 1949.

Curtis, Caroline and Mary Kawena Pukui.
"Hanakahi's Fishpond," *Tales of the Menehune.*
Honolulu, Hawai'i, Kamehameha Schools Press, 1960, p. 56.

Kirch, Patrick Vinton and Marion Kelly.
Prehistory and Ecology in a Windward Hawaiian Valley: Halawa Valley, Moloka'i.
Pacific Anthropological Records No. 24, Department of Anthropology, Honolulu, Bernice Pauahi Bishop Museum, 1975.

Marshall Kaplan, Gans, Kahn and Yamamoto.
Moloka'i Regional Development Plan: A Report to Maui Planning Commission, County of Maui.
Honolulu, 1979.

Meyer, Charles S.
Meyers and Moloka'i.
Alden, Iowa, Graphic-Agri Business, 1982.

Mooney, Ross L.
"Consider the Tree," *In Ways That Bring The Dawn.*
Kalamazoo, Michigan, Life Giving Enterprises, Inc., 1976, p. 15.

Neal, Marie C.
In Gardens of Hawai'i.
Bernice Pauahi Bishop Museum, Special Publication No. 50, Honolulu, B.P. Bishop Museum Press, 1965.

Parsons Brinkerhoff-Hirota Associates.
Water Resources Feasibility Study: Island of Moloka'i, Waikolu and Pelekunu Valleys.
Department of Land and Natural Resources, State of Hawai'i, 1969.

Pukui, Mary Kawena, Samuel H. Elbert, Esther T. Mookini.
Hawaiian-English Dictionary.
Honolulu, University Press of Hawai'i, 1971.

Pukui, Mary Kawena, Samuel H. Elbert, Esther T. Mookini.
Place Names of Hawai'i.
Honolulu, University Press of Hawai'i, 1974.

Schmitt, Robert C.
The Missionary Census of Hawai'i.
Pacific Anthropological Records No. 20, Department of Anthropology, Honolulu, Bernice Pauahi Bishop Museum, 1973.

Starbird, Ethel A.
"Moloka'i — Forgotten Hawai'i," *National Geographic,* Vol. 160, No. 2 (August, 1981), p. 188-219.

Stearns, Harold T. and Gordon A. MacDonald.
Geology and Ground Water Resources of the Island of Moloka'i, Hawai'i.
Territory of Hawai'i, Hawai'i Division of Hydrography, Bulletin II, 1947.

Summers, Catherine C.
Moloka'i: A Site Survey.
Pacific Anthropological Records No. 14, Department of Anthropology, Honolulu, Bernice Pauahi Bishop Museum, 1971.

Tinker, Spencer Wilkie.
Fishes of Hawai'i.
Honolulu, Hawaiian Service, Inc., 1978.

GLOSSARY

'aina momona
fruitful land

akule
fish, *trachiurops crumenophthalmus*

aloha
term of endearment, friendship, greeting

'ama'u
tree fern, *sadleria cyatheoides*, native

'apapane
Hawaiian honey creeper, *himatione sanguinea*, native

'aumakua
family or personal god

hala
pandanus odoratissimus, native

heiau
place of worship, temple

holoku
loose-fitting long dress introduced by missionaries

hula
Hawaiian dance

'ilima
shrub with delicate, commonly orange flowers used for *lei* or medicinal purposes, *sida fallax*, native

imu
underground oven

kahu kilo'ia
one who observes the movement of fish and directs fishermen

kahuna
one of skillful excellence in any profession

kahuna pule
priest, an expert in prayer

kalo
tuberous plant from which *poi* is made, the principal food of ancient Hawaiians, *colocasia esculenta*, native

kapa
paper cloth made from *wauke* or *mamaki* bark

kiawe
algaroba tree, *prosopis pallida*, exotic

kona
leeward side or wind

kukui
candlenut tree, *aleurites moluccana*, native

kuleana
ownership, right (as used in text)

lauhala
leaf of the *hala* tree, *pandanus odoratissimus*

lehua
blossom of the *'ohi'a-lehua* tree, *metrosideros collina*, native

lei
wreath of flowers, leaves, seeds or shells

limu
seaweed

limu kohu
specie of edible seaweed, *asparagopsis taxiformis*

lomi
to massage

lomi lomi salmon
favorite dish in Hawai'i

lu'au
Hawaiian feast, work usage dates from 19th century; *lit., taro* leaves

maile
forest vine with fragrant leaves used for *lei* and decoration, *alyxia olivaeformis*, native

maile lauli'ili'i
variety of *alyxia olivaeformis* growing on Moloka'i, native

make
to die

malama ka 'aina
to honor the land

mamaki
small tree, one of two sources of *kapa*, *pipturus albidus*, native

mana
spiritual power

mana'e
to the east, the East End of Moloka'i

mano
general name for shark

moi
fish, *polydactylus sexfilis*

mo'o
demigod who took the form of a lizard-like creature

mu'umu'u
loose-fitting dress

'ohana
family, extended family

'ohi'a-lehua
forest tree, *metrosideros polymorpha*, native

'opihi
Hawaiian limpet, *patella sandwichensis*

pali
cliff, precipice

paniolo
cowboy

pa'u
skirt worn by women horseback riders

pau hana
finished work

poi
staple Hawaiian food made from cooked, pounded *taro*

pu'uhonua
place of refuge

tapa
kapa

taro
kalo

'uala
sweet potato, *ipomoea batatas*, native

'ukulele
stringed instrument brought to Hawai'i by Portuguese in 1879; *lit.*, leaping flea

wahine
woman

wauke
paper mulberry tree, bark used to make *kapa*, *broussonetia papyrifera*, native

wiliwili
coral tree, cream to red blossom, *erythrina sandwichensis*, native

PHOTOGRAPHER'S ACKNOWLEDGEMENTS

Since first picking up a camera, I dreamed of this book. During the course of the project, I have been touched, supported and encouraged by many people. I would like to mention a few:

Co-publisher Bob Goodman was the first to review my collection of Moloka'i photographs, eight years ago. He saw the book that could emerge from my work and has remained true to that vision ever since.

Richard Cohn, Bob's partner in Beyond Words, shared his belief in the book's potential. When problems arose between us, it was Richard who, time and again, invited us to heal ourselves; to recommit to our common purpose.

Bronwyn Cooke, my wife and co-author, helped us create the "Joy Prospectus," which has become the foundation of Beyond Words Publishing Company. It is our contract with each other, and it follows in its entirety: "The freedom to be ourselves in the moment: expressing our feelings, and accepting our responsibility to listen, share and allow what is to be: this is crucial to all the rest." Bronwyn kept our focus clear throughout the editorial process, acting as a barometer of our feelings.

Jivan Mahasubh and Sangit Punitama have included Bronwyn and me not only in the design process, but as members of their family. They have taught us, fed us, and inspired us, while producing a design that is the expression of Moloka'i as we know her.

Over the years, the following people have given invaluable assistance in the development of our text, each offering their special talent and insight, helping to guide it toward completion: Misha Grudin, Gaines Smith, Tim Leigh, Joe Casey, Marilyn Musick, Phillip Spalding III, John Christensen, and Paul "Doc" Berry. Editor Liz Foster integrated the various contributions these individuals made and shaped our writing into its final form.

Dorothe Curtis guided us to many of the old archaeological sites and checked our manuscript for accuracy. With her husband Dave, she watched over our project for years.

Danny Kekahuna taught us many of the Hawaiian place names and their meanings. On numerous occasions, he shared the soul of Moloka'i through his music. Danny's wife, Louise, is another model of Hawaiian giving, whether with words, food, or the joy she brought with her incredible lauhala hats.

Dave Arnold, my first editor at *National Geographic*, gave me a crash course in photojournalism in 1980, when I covered Moloka'i. Tom Smith, also of *National Geographic*, helped obtain permission to reproduce five photographs used in their August 1981 issue.

With his enthusiasm for my photography, Phillip Spalding Jr., president of Molokai Ranch Ltd., has continued to be a motivating force behind the book. Mitz Watanabe, our "Moloka'i Manager," was always there when we needed him. Teijiro Oshiro helped keep our old Toyota Landcruiser mobile and he never failed to offer thoughtful, caring words.

Sandra Wolcott inevitably appeared with perfect timing to manifest solutions to the problems we faced, helping us accomplish our goals in a loving way. Out of friendship for us and his love for Moloka'i, Sam Cooke took the necessary steps which allowed this book to happen. Another valued friend, Paul Chesley, monitored the progress of the manuscript and layout, always reminding us to strive for our best. Cindy Black, Gail Michaels and our attorney David Williams added much to the joy of the process with their carefully considered advice on all levels of the book's creation. Chris Newbert helped us understand that process, leading the way with his book, *Within a Rainbowed Sea*.

My father and Vivian assisted us tremendously, providing a home base on Moloka'i from which we could photograph and write. My mother, Nancy Cooke de Herrera, encouraged my photography and supported our efforts to bring this book to completion in every way she could.

No list, however long, can contain all the names of those who have helped. On Moloka'i there are hundreds of people who, at one time or another, offered their friendship, wisdom and understanding. We want them to know that their gifts are appreciated. In giving to this book, they gave also to the island we love.

PUBLISHERS' ACKNOWLEDGEMENTS

The publishers would like to express their deep appreciation to all who have helped this book become a reality: Rikki Cooke, for his superb photographic ability and determination to honor the island of Moloka'i and her people through his work; Bronwyn Cooke, who wrote the "Joy Prospectus" and helped create Beyond Words Publishing Company; Cynthia Black and Gail Michaels, for their continued support and help in every aspect of the project; Liz Foster and Paul Berry, our friends and editors; David Hillman, for his careful proofreading; John Christensen, for his timely assistance; Meleana Pricher, for her photographic and editorial skills; Phil Spalding Jr., Peter Cumpston, Aka Hodgins and Gordon Lent of Molokai Ranch Limited, for their enthusiasm and belief in the book's potential; Phil Boydston of Kaluakoi Corporation and Louisiana Land Company, and Phil Spalding III, for their counsel; Connie Wright of Avatar, for her generosity and promotional efforts; Rubelite Johnson, for her expertise in the Hawaiian language and culture; Dorothe Curtis, for her contribution to the book in fact and spirit; Tony Hodges and Life of the Land, for his friendship and the creative concept "books that plant trees"; Rick Reiner and the staff at Hawaiian One Hour Color Photo; the editor and staff of *Islands*; Sam Cooke, for his support; Fred M. Murrell and Rosalyn Voget, for opening their homes; Jeff and Andy Alexander, for their early help in organizing the project; Jivan Mahasubh and Sangit Punitama and their staff of dedicated designers; Char and Byron Liske, Dave Sengenberger and all the people at Dynagraphics, for their incredible dedication and service to the dream of The EarthSong Collection; Dwight and Karen Cummings and their team at Wy'east Color, who have applied their color separation skills to every image of the book; "Biff" Atwater, Fred Dempsey and S.D. Warren, for the timely arrival of their Lustro Gloss Enamel paper; Dale Simonsen, Dave Rhodes and John Reeder at Zellerbach Paper Company, for their technical support; John Thomas and Bud Kennedy, for their superb typography; Bob Bengtson and Lynn Sutcliff at Lincoln and Allen, our bookbinders; Al C. Nieman and Marty Sychowski of Bowers Printing Inks; Mike Clarizio of Spectrum Inks; Dirk Liepelt, Liepelt & Son Printers; Jan Turner of Weyerhaeuser Company; Bob Millsap and Tom Zwald of U.S. National Bank of Oregon; Bill Breeden, Bank of Hawaii; Allan Fulsher of Bauer, Winfree, Anderson, Fountain and Schaub; Henry Blauer of Laventhol and Horwath; Hans Schroeder of Hans Schroeder Accounting;

Tim Girvin, for his brilliant calligraphy; Marilyn Musick, for her editorial assistance; Jesus Sanchez, our gifted limited edition bookbinder; Marcia Morse, for her highly creative papermaking; Keith Haugen, for his willingness to help; Tom Smith of *National Geographic*; Rick Davis of Davick Publications; Rita Gormley of *Aloha*; Tim Evard and James Chiddix of Oceanic Cablevision Inc. in Honolulu; Buck Buchwach, George Chaplin and Thurston Twigg-Smith of the *Honolulu Advertiser*; Mr. Tetsuo Hirasawa and Mike Matzkin of Canon U.S.A.; Cornell Capa of The International Center of Photography in New York City; Sean Callahan and Erla Zwingle of *American Photographer*; Rich Peck of Peck Sims Mueller, Inc., for his friendship and advertising skills; Gordon Hess of Litho-Color (Hawai'i); Jonathan Rinehart of Adams and Rinehart, New York; Mr. Harry Hoffman, President of Waldenbooks; Bonnie Predd, Pam Origi, John Zales, Howard Jones and Inger Otter of the Waldenbooks executive staff; Sandra Richardson, Marshall May, Frank Pastorini and Barbara Hood of the Ted Colangelo Agency; and Les Sinclair, Executive Producer, Merv Griffin Productions. Last, but far from least, our investors: David and Dorothy Cohn, Fred M. Murrell, Richard and Laurie Humphrey, The Oregon Mountain Community, Cynthia Maloney Inc., Cynthia Black, Sherrill MacNaughton, Bill Weyerhaeuser, Don Granger, Nancy Cooke de Herrera, Molokai Ranch Limited, Adrian and Carol Adams, Casey and Linda Albright, Marcia Duff, Gary D. Peters, and Bea Stern.